USA

Hilary Bunce

Macdonald Educational

Seattle

Missouri River

Snake River

Great Salt Lake

Colorado River

San Francisco

GOLDEN NUGGET
CASINO

Denver

River Arkansas

Los Angeles

MEXICO

Rio Grande

Pacific Ocean

Alaska

Hawaii

Scale

0   100   200   300   400 mi

0   100   200   300   400 km

CANADA

Lake Superior

Minneapolis

Lake Huron

Lake Michigan

Lake Ontario

Hudson River

Boston

Detroit

Lake Erie

Chicago

Pittsburgh

New York

Philadelphia

Baltimore

Washington

St. Louis

River Mississippi

Atlanta

Atlantic Ocean

Dallas

Houston

New Orleans

Bahama Islands

Map of the
United States of America

CUBA

Contents

From the sunny orange groves of California in the West to the industrial East, the United States of America is a huge country. Britain would fit into it over 40 times. There are 50 states in the Union. Hawaii and Alaska are a very long way from the other 48 states. The government in Washington DC makes national laws but each state can make its own laws too.

The land of America is as varied as its people. Americans come from Europe, Africa, Asia and Latin America. Many of them keep some of the customs they had in the 'Old Country'. But speaking English unites them. And they are proud that their children grow up as Americans.

Many people went to the New World to find work and freedom. Let's have a look at the land they chose for their new life.

At school

If you went to school in the United States you would probably find it very different from your own school. Many schools are large, with plenty of grounds for sports. The school would have a large hall with the American flag on a pole at the front. The pupils would be wearing their own comfortable clothes – there is no school uniform.

Most American adults start work early in the morning. So do children. They get up at 6.30am in time to shower and eat a big breakfast.

School begins at 8 o'clock and lessons continue until 2.30 or 3pm. Most schools in America are free; parents do not have to pay for their children to learn. The pupils learn much the same things as you do but often spend more time at sports such as basketball, tennis, baseball and American football. Older children also learn things like typing, how to drive a car – and even rollerskating!

Some children bring a packed lunch from home while others can buy food in the school canteen. But there is no proper lunch hour. Pupils eat when they have some spare time.

As school finishes early, many older children take a job in the afternoon. They may work in shops, cafés or gas (petrol) stations and earn money for the vacation (holiday).

At Christmas and Easter school vacations usually last one week. In the North the school might be closed during the winter because of snow and then there is no Easter vacation at all. But everyone looks forward to the nine-week-long summer break, even if some continue to go to school. This is called 'summer school' and gives the children a chance to study things they may not have had time to learn during the term. They can take classes in art or sport or music.

Many American children stay for a few weeks of the summer at Summer Camp. Much of their time is spent out of doors.

Big yellow bus! Most children get a free bus ride to school in the School Bus.

American classes are called *grades*. At the age of six children begin in the 1st Grade. If they stay at school until they are 18 they will be in the 12th Grade.

Children between the ages of six and ten go to Elementary or 'Grade' school. From 11 to 14 they go to Junior High and from 15 to 18 Senior High. At Senior High the pupils have special names depending on which grade they are in. They begin in the 9th Grade as *Freshmen* and then become *Sophomores*. 11th Graders are called *Juniors* and 12th Graders *Seniors*.

At the end of the school year is a big ceremony for the Seniors called Graduation. The departing Seniors wear caps and gowns and receive a certificate. The whole family gathers proudly to hear speeches. Many children are given big presents by their parents. They also receive a copy of their school's yearbook. This has a photograph of each graduate and says what they want to do after they have left school.

Every morning, in every US school the pledge of allegiance *is taken. The children promise loyalty to their flag and country.*

Universal Film Studios in Hollywood. Visitors hang on as they cross the collapsing bridge. But don't worry, the bridge will be ready for the next train-load of tourists!

California

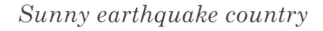

More people live in California than in any other state. Much of the coast is built up like a long, thin city. People came to California in search of sunshine and gold. The gold is gone but the sun still drenches the rich land that slopes into the warm, blue Pacific Ocean.

Much of the land was once a great desert. But engineers have built giant dams, like the Hoover Dam, which re-route rivers to water the barren desert. Fruit like oranges, peaches and grapes grows here now. Americans say that if you spit on the desert a flower will grow – they were right about California!

Sometimes the earth grumbles menacingly. This is a land of earthquakes. Occasionally a big one rips open the rock, just like the one that

A tram speeds down one of the San Francisco hills. In the icy bay Alcatraz Prison – almost impossible to escape from – clings to a rock. It is now a tourist attraction.

Surfing USA! A daring surfer skims his board across the Pacific Ocean rollers.

destroyed San Francisco in 1906. San Francisco was rebuilt and is now one of America's loveliest cities. But people are always waiting for the next earthquake!

After New York, Los Angeles is America's largest city. It is not really one city but about 50 small towns joined into one big 80 kilometre-wide sprawl. If you 'phone across town, you pay long-distance rates!

Los Angeles is a city of cars. Highways, gas stations and parking lots (car parks) cover almost a third of the city's area. Traffic jams and exhaust fumes are a menace. Smoke and fog mix together into a filthy brown cloud called smog. A thick blanket of smog can choke the city so that even the bright sun becomes invisible. But that's what happens when 3 million people own 3½ million cars.

Nearby you can visit the Hollywood film studios. On a pavement outside a cinema you can see the concrete hand- and footprints and autographs of many film stars. The first film-makers came to Hollywood in 1912 to film in the year-round sunshine. Today people prefer television to the cinema and now Los Angeles is more important for making aircraft, cars and tyres than films.

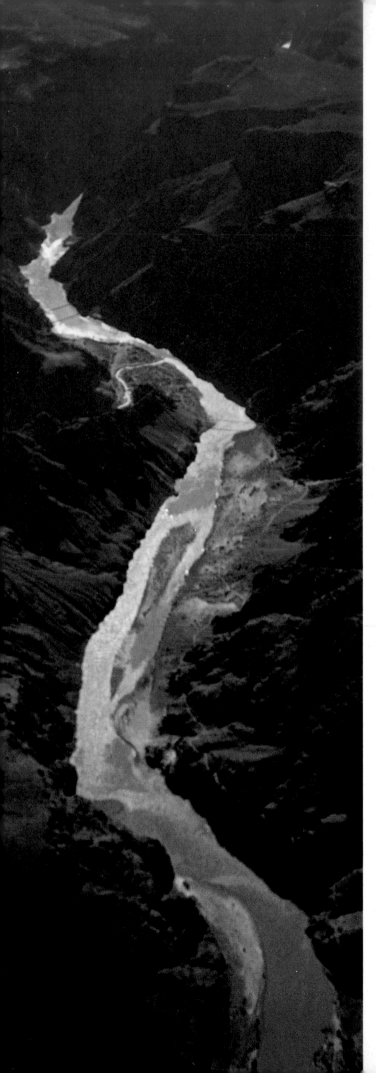

Wonders of the New World

America is a land of contrasts. Beyond the sprawling cities lie huge areas of great beauty. These places are called National Parks. The government has preserved the countryside as it was when Europeans first set foot in the New World.

In Yellowstone Park in Wyoming rugged mountain peaks surround hot soda springs and steamy geysers. Every hour Old Faithful – the most famous geyser – shoots up huge jets of steaming water. Animals like elk, moose, black bears, chipmunks and buffalo live in the park, protected from hunters.

Giant redwood trees grow in Northern California and Oregon. Many of them are 3,000 years old. They are so tall it's hard to see their tops. A hole was once cut in a redwood trunk. There was enough room for a car to drive right through the middle of the tree!

The Niagara Falls tumble between Canada and the United States. They are the world's second biggest waterfall. The power from the falling water is used to generate electricity for many local industries.

Towering 18 metres at Mount Rushmore, South Dakota are the faces of four American presidents. They have been carved from the cliff rocks. Alfred Hitchcock once made a frightening film here. The stars had to escape by climbing down the faces!

Stalagmites and stalactites make fairy-land shapes in New Mexico's Carlsbad Caverns. At sunset a huge black cloud rises from the caves. The cloud is made of bats. Every evening they go out to hunt for insects. As many as 5,000 bats a minute blast out of the cavern into the night.

In the Arizona Desert the Colorado River surges through Grand Canyon over 1 km from the clifftop.

The sun scorches Monument Valley, Utah. Many cowboy movies have been made among the rocky outcrops.

Out on the open range

The West

The American West starts at the Mississippi River. Apart from the few big towns like Los Angeles and Houston, people live a long way from each other. Fast highways, planes, radio and TV help people to keep in touch. But not long ago the West was a vast unexplored area.

Explorers and trappers were the first people to set foot in this wild country. But in 1848 gold was discovered in California. The 'gold rush' began. Hundreds of people raced west in search of fortune. Their journeys were long and dangerous. They used guns to fight off enemies in order to claim the fertile land they found as

One combine harvester isn't enough! More wheat is grown on the Prairies than anywhere else in the world.

their own. Many Americans still carry guns today. They believe they have a right to do so as part of their history.

Early pioneers found huge herds of cattle. Realising they could sell meat and leather to the Eastern cities they stayed. To work on the land you needed tough clothes. Denim jeans and cowboy boots come from America's West. The cowboy's life was hard and dangerous. On the long trails they had to fight wild beasts, unfriendly Indians, harsh weather and farmers who had settled the land.

Americans were the first people to put food in cans (tins). Chicago began as a big meat packing centre. Chicagoans say that they eat what they can and can what they can't. But a way of preserving meat in ice in railway wagons was invented and Chicago's meat-canning trade gave way to iron and steel and televisions.

The cattle auctioneer rattles out his patter so fast that only the farmers can understand him. Millions of head of cattle are sold in this way each year.

American Indians

American Indians still bake bread in the traditional way in clay ovens out of doors.

American Indians were the first Americans. About 35,000 years ago they crossed from Asia into Alaska and moved southwards into North and South America. When Christopher Columbus arrived in America from Europe in 1492 he made a big mistake. He thought he had reached India. So he called the people he saw 'Indians'.

There were hundreds of tribes, living all over America. Over half the American states still have Indian names. They spoke about 2,000 different languages, wore different clothes and built different homes. Only the white people thought of them all as 'Indians'. Many did not even know of each other's existence. When the Polar Eskimos first saw white people in 1818 they were very surprised. They thought they were the only people on earth!

The many tribes used the huge areas of land in different ways. The Iroquois in the North-East were farmers and hunters. They settled in one place and built dome-shaped houses from bent poles. They grew maize and pumpkins and collected maple syrup from the trees. The Iroquois may have been the people with whom the Pilgrim Fathers ate the first harvest meal. Today this is remembered by all Americans every Thanksgiving Day. The Catawba tribe in the South grew cotton long before it became 'king' in the 19th century.

The nomadic tribes needed homes which could easily be moved. The Crow tribe of the Central Plains hunted the great herds of buffalo in the summer. They would pitch tents, or teepees, covered in buffalo hide near the herds.

It was the Pueblo Indians of the South-West who, in the 15th century, built the earliest homes in America. Some of them still survive. They were like huge apartment blocks built of sun-baked bricks. They had up to 800 rooms. Over 1,000 people could live in the type of building that white Americans would only be able to build 500 years later in New York City.

When white people first arrived most Indians were friendly. They traded their skins for the knives and beads which the white people had brought with them from Europe. But the white people wanted land. They moved further and further westwards, taking the Indians' land. The Indians had to fight hard to keep their land but there were more whites and they had more guns. The Indians were finally defeated in 1890 at the Battle of Wounded Knee. Thousands had been killed and many buffalo herds had been wiped out. This left the Indians with no way of getting food.

Today many Indians live on reservations. These are pieces of land given to them by the government. But much of this land is poor and many Indians do not have jobs. Some people are trying to make the Indians' lives better. But their plight is a sad fact of American history.

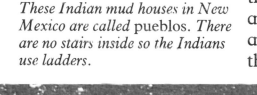

These Indian mud houses in New Mexico are called pueblos. *There are no stairs inside so the Indians use ladders.*

Indian crafts

Indian culture is very close to nature. Today many Indians are Christians but they have not forgotten their old religions and gods. They believed the Earth was their mother. The Sun and the Thunderbird, the Raingod and the Rainbow Man were some of their gods. And in their crafts they use the things they see in nature.

Indians who lived in woods or by the sea drew birds and animals. Desert Indians used geometrical designs in earthy colours – red, black, yellow and white. Pueblo Indians still decorate their clay pots with pictures of birds and turtles. They are famous for their silver jewellery with flower patterns of turquoise stones. White people first gave Indians beads. With these they decorated their clothes with beautiful leaf and animal patterns.

When a Navajo is ill the medicine man makes pictures of the Navajo gods from coloured sand. They ask the gods to make that person better. Sometimes they ask for a good harvest too. They also use *ojos de dios* which means god's eyes.

Ojos are two sticks with coloured wool twined round to look like an eye. Indians use them to ask for a god's protection.

Today many Indian crafts are made just for tourists. But Indian children still learn to make *ojos* in school. Why don't you try too?

Will the ojos *tied to the ponies' tails help them to win?*

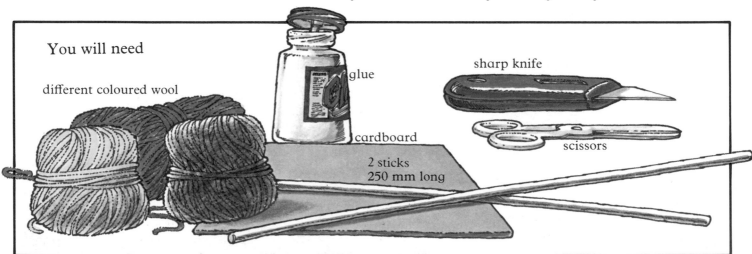

You will need

different coloured wool

glue

sharp knife

cardboard

scissors

2 sticks
250 mm long

Make an ojo

1. Ask an adult to cut a notch in the middle of each stick. Glue them together to form a cross. Wait until the glue dries.

2. Tie the wool to the middle of the cross. Begin wrapping the wool tightly to make the 'eye'. Go over and around each stick. Glue a few centimetres ahead of you along each stick.

3. Cut the yarn off and tie it with a single knot. Leave a 4 cm end. Glue this to the stick and work over it. Always end a colour on the same stick on which it began.

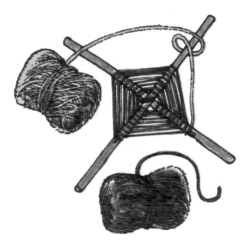

4. Tie a new colour on to a different stick. Leave a 4 cm end and glue it down the stick.

5. If you want to make a space between colours wrap the wool round and round the stick. Knot it and do the same on the other sticks. Then tie on a new colour.

6. Leave the ends of the sticks bare. Make 2 tassels to finish off your ojo. Wrap wool round and round the card.

7. Cut at one end and take out the card. Tie a piece of wool round the top. Then tie your tassels on the ends of your ojo.

8. Try making other ojos in different sizes and colours. Perhaps you can invent other ways of wrapping the wool round the sticks. Hang the ojo up. Maybe it will bring you luck!

The Lone Star State

Texas

Texans have a saying: 'Big is beautiful.' Until Alaska joined the Union in 1959 Texas was the biggest state. Both Alaskans and Texans boast of the size of their states, their wealth and their oil. Texas is so big Britain would fit into it three times.

Over 14 million people live in Texas but the vast ranches contain even more cattle. Amarillo is the centre of the cattle industry. Every year four million cows arrive at Amarillo's huge feed lots.

Room to move! Freeways and parking lots have taken over land in Dallas where cattle once used to roam.

Cowboy traditions live on at the many rodeos held in Texas. This bucking bronco is in the huge Houston Astrodome. The floor is covered with fake grass called Astroturf.

The myth of the cowboy lingers here. Many people still wear cowboy boots and stetsons or 'ten-gallon' hats even if they work in the city. More people now live in cities than cattle ranches and more people earn their living from oil than from meat. Houston is the centre of Texas' oil industry. It is America's fastest growing city. Over 1,000 people move there each week.

Almost 2½ million Mexican Americans live in Texas. The state was once a part of Mexico. Now the Rio Grande – which is Spanish for 'big river' – forms part of the border between Mexico and the United States. Spanish is almost as common as English.

Mexican *chilli* (spicy hot meat and beans) and *tacos* (crispy meat-filled corn pancakes) are as popular as beans and barbecue beef, the traditional cowboy fare. But the meal you will come across all over Texas is the massive, succulent steak with cold Lone Star beer. Texas is called the Lone Star State. The single star on its flag dates from 1836–1845 when Texas was independent from the Union.

Why cowboys sing in Texas

Today cowboys sing in Texas. They sing, "Yippeeyi!" And they sing, "Yippeeyay!" But it wasn't always so. Long ago cowboys didn't sing. Cowboys were silent then. And the most silent of them all was Slim Jim.

Once, in Texas, in that old silent time, Slim Jim was guarding a herd of cattle at night. It was a long dark night and Slim Jim was lonely.

"I wish I could hear a little noise," he thought. "Any kind of noise that wouldn't frighten the cows."

Slim Jim knew that if anything frightened the cows they'd stampede. They'd stampede and run all over Texas. It might take a month of Sundays to round them up again. Slim Jim thought of the noise he'd like to hear. It was a song.

"Just a little song wouldn't frighten the cows," he said.

So Slim Jim opened his mouth and sang. The song woke the cows. They didn't like it. They couldn't stand that song. Big ones and little ones, spotted ones and plain ones, all the cows stampeded. They stampeded all over Texas.

Slim Jim and the other cowboys rode out to round up the cows. They rode through the mesquite with its long straight thorns. They rode through the Spanish dagger with its long sharp spikes. They rode through the cats-claw with its long curved briars. And they rode through the clumps of cactus with its long prickly needles. But the thorns did not hurt them. And the spikes and briars and needles did not hurt them. Because they wore leather cowboy chaps on their legs.

Slim Jim was the best rider and the best rope in all Texas. But it took him and the other cowboys half a month of Sundays to round up those cows.

"Now listen," the other cowboys said to Slim Jim. "No more singing in Texas."

"Boys," Slim Jim said, "I can't promise. It's lonely at night on this prairie. That song keeps running through my mind. And I have to sing it."

Then Slim Jim got on his horse. "I'll go far away. I'll find a place where there are no cows to be frightened by my singing." And he rode away.

By and by Slim Jim came to a river. It was a very dry, dusty river. It was the Rio Grande. But there were fish in a little water out in the middle.

"Hm," thought Slim Jim, "a tasty fish would make a fine supper." But Slim Jim was a cowboy not a fisherman. He had no fishhooks and he had no fishline. But Slim Jim was the finest roper in all Texas. So he whirled his rope and he roped a fish. Slim Jim camped on the river bank and cooked his fish.

It was lonely there, beside the river. Slim Jim's song kept running through his mind. He opened his mouth and he sang that song. And his song didn't frighten the fish in the Rio Grande. Not a single fish stampeded.

"This is the place for me," said Slim Jim. "I shall stay here and sing, and be a fisherman." So he threw away his leather cowboy chaps and he stayed beside the river. And he fished. And he sang.

But while Slim Jim fished and sang there was trouble in Texas. The other cowboys remembered Slim Jim's song. They just couldn't help it. They sang that song.

And the cows didn't like it. They couldn't stand that song. Big ones and little ones, spotted ones and plain ones, they all stampeded. They stampeded all over Texas. The cowboys rode for a whole month of Sundays. But they couldn't get the cows rounded up again.

Then up spoke Cactus Pete of the Pecos country.

"Boys," he said, "Slim Jim is the best cowboy in all Texas. We must get him to help us round up those cows." And the other cowboys agreed. So they rode out to find Slim Jim.

They rode all over Texas until they came to the Rio Grande.

And they found Slim Jim fishing.

"Cows are stampeding all over Texas," they told him. "You must help us round up those cows."

Slim turned away from the river. "Slim Jim will ride and round 'em up," he cried. "All you cowboys follow me."

So Slim Jim rode to round up the cows. He rode through those thorny bushes, and Slim Jim felt the thorns. He felt them because he wasn't wearing the leather cowboy chaps he laid aside when he became a fisherman.

When he felt the mesquite thorns Slim Jim shouted, "Yip!" When he felt the Spanish dagger spikes he shouted, "Yippee!" When he felt the cactus needles he shouted, "Yi!" When he felt the cats-claw briars he shouted, "Yay!" And when he felt them all at the same time, Slim Jim shouted, "Yipee yi, yippee yay!"

Everywhere that Slim Jim rode the cows heard him. They liked those new sounds that Slim Jim made. They stopped to listen to Jim's yips and yippees and yis and yays. Then up spoke Cactus Pete of Pecos country.

"Slim Jim," said he, "the cows like those yippeeyi noises. Make those noises again, Slim."

So Slim Jim did. He made a tune out of the noises. The cows liked the new song. Big ones and little ones, spotted ones and plain ones, they all stopped to listen. Then Slim Jim and the other cowboys rounded them up. And that was the end of the big stampede in Texas.

And that's why cowboys sing today in Texas. They sing, "Yippeeyi!" and they sing, "yippeeyay!" They sing Slim Jim's song in Texas.

The Mississippi

Long before white people came to live in America tribes of Indians lived along a great river. They called it Misi Sipi which means 'big water'. It was a good name. For from its source in the North to its delta in the Gulf of Mexico the Mississippi is 3,800 km long.

Many different boats have sailed the Mississippi in its long history. The Indians and French fur trappers used canoes and rafts. Later came flatboats and keelboats with sails. But the most famous river boats were the 19th century paddle steamers. They carried cargo and passengers between New Orleans and Minneapolis.

The Mississippi divides the United States into East and West. But it is an important waterway for transporting goods between North and South. Huge oil refineries line the river around Baton Rouge. To refine one barrel of crude oil you need about 7,300 litres of water. And the Mississippi provides enough water to refine 340,000 barrels a day – and enough to transport the oil. Tankers carry it upstream to the North. They pass pilot ships pushing huge groups of barges called tows coming downstream. These carry coal, grain, steel and cars and they return with cargoes of cotton, sugar and coffee. Transporting goods by water is much cheaper than by road or rail.

Three big cities stand on the banks of the Mississippi. Minneapolis in the North lies on the edge of the wheat country. The grain is sent

A floating palace. The luxurious Mississippi steamboats used to race each other up the river. Sometimes their boilers exploded and hundreds of people were drowned when the boats sank.

A funeral procession winds its way through the French Quarter of New Orleans. Jazz musicians play in the streets on the way back from the cemetery expressing the great emotion they feel on this sad occasion.

to the city to be ground into flour. At St Louis the muddy Missouri joins the blue Mississippi and turns its waters brown. The Missouri is the biggest of the twelve great rivers which flow into the Mississippi. It rises 4,000 km away in the Rocky Mountains.

New Orleans, the birthplace of jazz, is the most colourful city in the States. Houses with intricate iron balconies date from the time the French and Spanish lived there. At night tap dancers perform in the streets and jazz musicians play in Preservation Hall. And every February the whole town comes alive for the famous Mardi Gras carnival. For many days and nights there are floats, bands and fancy dress parties. Thousands of people throng to the city to dance in the streets.

Be bop a lula

All over the world children listen to popular American music. In America itself you can hear it everywhere – in hotel lobbies (foyers), shops and bars.

An important feature of pop music is its strong beat. Pop has its roots in the music of American negroes who were taken from Africa to work as slaves in the South. Much African music is based on the beat of drums. The songs the slaves sang in the hot cotton fields to make their hard work seem easier mingled with the spirituals they sang in church. This mixture gradually became the *blues*. Black musicians travelled from town to town singing the blues. They sang of the hard, poor lives they led. City blues developed into *rhythm and blues*.

After the Civil War last century, black musicians began to play the same brass

Country and Western music began with cowboy folk songs and is popular among white people in the West. Anybody can be invited to join in.

Jazz is a mesh of complex melodies and rhythms. The music is not written down. Inspired by each other, the musicians can make it up as they go along.

instruments as the soldiers had in the war. In New Orleans their music was spiced with that of the French and Spanish Creole people. The result was *jazz*. Jazz travelled up the Mississippi and then all over the world.

Pop music as we know it began in the 1950s. White people adapted rhythm and blues to produce *rock 'n' roll*. The first person to do this successfully was a poor white truck driver called Elvis Presley. Before he died in 1977 over 250 million copies of his records had been sold. His songs are still loved everywhere but when he first started singing some people hated his music and even smashed his records!

Earlier this century, many 'serious' composers, too, were impressed by the 'new' sounds of jazz. When the Russian composer Stravinsky arrived in America in the 1920s he was influenced by these sounds and rhythms and began to put them into his compositions. But some people didn't like it. New music almost always has its critics before people get used to it and accept it.

The old South

The southern states of America are hot and sticky. Alligators live in the steamy swamps and murky rivers. When white people went to live in the southern states of America they planted tobacco, rice and cotton. Slaves were brought from Africa to work on the tobacco and cotton plantations. These slaves are the ancestors of America's black people.

Slaves were the property of their masters. They were bought and sold just like cattle. The rich slave-owners lived in mansions called plantation houses. These were very different from the shabby and crowded cabins in which the slaves were forced to live.

By the mid-19th century many people in the northern states had decided that slavery was wrong. They wanted slaves to be free. In 1860

Surrounded by fronds of Spanish moss hanging from shady trees, this Southern mansion is today a museum. The rich plantation - and slave-owners lived in houses like this.

Dr Martin Luther King was a peaceful campaigner for Black civil rights during the 1950s and 1960s. But he was a victim of the violence he hated. He was assassinated in 1968 in Memphis, Tennessee.

Abraham Lincoln was elected President. He promised to end slavery. But in the South the landowners depended on the slaves to work the huge plantations. So in 1861 the southern states declared themselves independent from the North and civil war broke out. For four years there were bloody battles. Half a million people were killed. In 1865 the North won and the South returned to the Union. The slaves were freed.

But life in the South was very difficult for the freed blacks. Few had much money or education. They still worked the land but often had to give most of their crops to the landowner. Sometimes they did not have enough food for their own families. Many white southern farmers were poor, too. The war had ruined their land.

For many years the South remained a poor area. There was little money and the pace of life was slow. Southerners still speak slowly with a drawl which is difficult for a Yankee (Northerner) to understand. Many whites tried to make sure that the blacks stayed weak and poor. The whites were so powerful that the blacks were prevented from voting. This was a right which had been granted after the Civil War. They stopped them going to school, burned their homes and even killed some of them.

Until the 1950s blacks had to lead separate lives from whites. They could not use the same cinemas, buses or schools. In courtrooms they were made to swear the oath on separate bibles. The blacks fought long and hard to get the vote. And although segregation is illegal nowadays, there are still some white people who do not want the blacks to have the same rights as them.

The slaves working on the big plantations used to spend their evenings round a fire outside their poor cabins. They would tell each other stories in the language they had developed. One of their favourite characters was Brer Rabbit.

Brer Rabbit secures a mansion

It turn out one time long ago dat a whole lot o' de creeturs took a notion dat dey get together an' build a house. Ole Brer Bear, an' Brer Fox, an' Brer Wolf, an' Brer Racoon, an' Brer Possum. An' it seem like Brer Mink was among 'em too. Well, dey whirl in an' dey buil' de house in less'n no time.

Brer Rabbit, he make out he get dizzy up on de scaffolding. An' he say he can't see if he work in de sun. But he got him a ruler an' stuck a pencil behin' his ear, an' he go round measurin' an' markin' – measurin' an' markin'. An' he was dat busy dat de other creeturs think he doin' a monstrous sight o' work. An' folks goin' along de road say Brer Rabbit doin' more hard work dan de whole lot o' dem. Yet all de time Brer Rabbit ain't doin' nothin' – he might as well be layin' in de shade scratchin' hisself. De other creeturs, dey buil' de house.

She was a fine house, too. She bin a fine house these days, let alone those days. She had a upstairs an' a downstairs an' chimbleys all round, an' she had enough rooms for all de creeturs.

Brer Rabbit, he pick out a nice upstairs room. An' he went an' got 'im a gun, an' a big brass cannon. An' when de other creeturs weren't looking, he put 'em in his room. An' he get a tub of nasty slop-water, an' he put dat in when dey weren't looking. So, when dey got de house all fix, all de creeturs was a-sittin' in de parlour after supper. Brer Rabbit, he stretch hisself an' make excuses an' say he believe he'll go to his room. When he get der, an' while all de other creeturs was a-laughin' an a-chattin', Brer Rabbit, he stick his head out of de room an' sing out,

"When a big man like me wanter sit down, wharbouts he goin' to sit?" sezee.

De other creeturs dey laugh an' holler back,

"If a big man like you can't sit in a chair, he better sit on de floor!"

"Watch out down der, den," sez ole Brer Rabbit, sezee. "'Cause I'm goin' to sit down," sezee.

With that – *bang* went the gun! Of course this sort of astonish de other creeturs an' dey look at one another much as to say,

"What in de name of gracious is dat?" Dey listen an' listen but don't hear no more fuss.

By an' by Brer Rabbit stick his head out of de room an' sing out,

"When a big man like me wanter sneeze, wharbouts he goin' to sneeze?" sezee. De other creeturs holler back,

"If a big man like you ain't gone crazy, he can sneeze anywhere he please."

"Watch out down der, den," says Brer Rabbit, sezee. "'Cause I'm a-goin' to sneeze right here," sezee.

With that Brer Rabbit let off his cannon – *bulderum-m-m*! De window glass rattled an' de house shook like she goin' to fall down – an' ole Brer Bear, he fell out of his rocking chair – *kerblump!* When de creeturs get settled, Brer Possum an' Brer Mink say dat Brer Rabbit got such a monstrous bad cold dey believe dey'll step out an' get some fresh air. But de other creeturs say dey goin' to stick it out. An' after a while when dey get der hair smoothed down, dey begin to chat again. An' Brer Rabbit, he sing out,

"When a big man like me wanter chew terbacker, wharbouts he goin' to spit?" An' de other creeturs holler back like dey were mad,

"Big man or little man, spit where you please!" Den Brer Rabbit, he squeal out,

"Dis is de way a big man spit!"

An' with that he tilt over de tub of slop-water. An' when de other creeturs hear it come a-sloshin' down de stairs, well dey just ran out o' der. Some of dem went out de back door, an' some of dem went out de front door, an' some of dem fell out de windows. Some went one way an' some went de other but dey all went sailing out.

An' Brer Rabbit, he just fasten de windows, an' shut up de house an' den he go to bed. An' he pull de covers up round his ears an' he sleep like a man what don't owe nobody nothin'. An' he don't owe dem nothin' 'cause if dem other creeturs goin' to get scared an' run off from der own house, what business is dat of Brer Rabbit? Dat's what he like to know.

The new South

Today the South is changing fast. After many years of poverty people are moving in. Some of the black people who left when the South was poor and hostile have returned. It is easier to find work. Air conditioning has made the intense heat more bearable. Industry is now established.

Steel plants pour out molten metal night and day in Birmingham, Alabama. Cargo ships dock in New Orleans while oil rigs drilling off the Louisiana shores supply some of the constant demand for petrol.

Alligators lurk in the swampy Florida Everglades. Tourists are taken in boats to spot them.

Atlanta, Georgia, is a big business centre. Huge office towers of shiny glass line the main street. More black people than white live in Atlanta and the city has had a black mayor since 1973. America's most famous drink, Coca Cola, was born there in 1886. Now 250 million Coke drinks are produced every day throughout the world.

But agriculture is still important. At the turn of the century the boll weevil, an insect, devastated the cotton crops. So Southerners had to find other crops to plant. Cotton is still grown but now there are peanuts and soybeans too. Jimmy Carter owns a large peanut farm. When he became President in 1976 people called him 'the peanut President'. If you see someone smoking a cigarette it probably came from Virginia or North Carolina. And Florida orange juice is drunk in many countries.

Many rich old people spend their last years in Florida. It is never cold so they can sit on the warm beaches all year round. Some of them live in retirement villages. No children are allowed – the old people like peace and quiet!

The car is king

This Ford production line helps to swell the vast number of motor vehicles on US roads. There are over 120 million cars registered in the US!

Have you heard the saying that Americans use their cars just to drive round the block? Sometimes this is true! The car really is king: there is more than one car for every two people.

In the early days only rich people could afford a car. But then in Detroit a man called Henry Ford decided that ordinary people should have cars too. In 1908 he designed a now-famous car – the Model T Ford. It was cheap because it was manufactured on an assembly line instead of being made by hand. Ford said that people could have any colour they wanted, as long as it was black! Ford is now one of the world's leading car makers. And so many vehicles are manufactured in Detroit that it is called 'Motor City'.

A great road system of wide highways was built but problems came with having so many vehicles. The big cars of which Americans were

so fond used up too much of the increasingly scarce gas. So powerful 'gas guzzlers' have given way to smaller cars. City air has become choked with pollution and great areas of land are covered with giant scrap heaps.

Because Americans are so dependent on their cars and there is so much space they invented the drive-in. You can spend almost the entire day in your car: in the morning you may draw some money at a drive-in bank. Shopping will probably be done at an enormous supermarket at the edge of town. You park in front and once the goods have been paid for someone will carry them back to the car. Lunch might be a burger from a drive-in restaurant. And for entertainment you could try the drive-in movie, an open air cinema. Hundreds of cars can park in front of a huge screen and listen through a loudspeaker. Travelling in the States will probably mean staying in a motel which is a drive-in hotel with cabins. The car is parked right outside your room.

You don't even have to leave your car to pray! At this drive-in church the preacher gives a sermon over a loudspeaker.

Eat American!

Every region and every group of people in the States has its special food. In New England there is fish soup called clam chowder; in New York, Jewish bagels and lox – smoked salmon rolls; in the South you'll find Negro food like grits – a kind of corn porridge – and cornbread; in the South-West, chilli, tacos and refried beans from Mexico. And in cattle country there are juicy T-bone steaks. But the one meal that you find all over the States is, of course, the hamburger and Coke.

All over the country there are plenty of smart restaurants and local dishes. But an American family can also travel over 4,000 km and still find the same chain restaurant they have back home, making food to the same standard. McDonald's golden arches, the beaming Colonel of Kentucky Fried Chicken and the HoJo (Howard Johnson's) spire loom up in every corner of America.

In America you can eat fast and eat big. This is the land of the Big Mac and Jumbo Jack hamburger; the three-scoop ice cream; the pizza big enough for 15 people. Americans often eat out, even breakfast. They expect good, fast service. And they usually get it. As you leave a restaurant someone always says, 'Have a nice day.'

Make brownies

You will need

1 teaspoon vanilla essence

75 gm sugar

some milk

greased baking tray 200 mm square

100 gm flour

glass bowl in saucepan of water

sieve

75 gm shelled walnuts

wooden spoon

75 gm plain chocolate

mixing bowl

75 gm butter or margarine

1 beaten egg

$\frac{1}{4}$ teaspoon baking powder

chopping board

$\frac{1}{4}$ teaspoon salt

knife

oven gloves

1. Turn on the oven to Gas 4, 350°F. Chop the walnuts on a board. The pieces should be about a centimetre big.

2. Beat the butter and sugar in a bowl with a wooden spoon. It looks white and creamy when it is ready.

3. Pour in the beaten egg bit by bit. Beat after each time. Then sift in the flour, salt and baking powder. Stir.

4. Melt chocolate in a bowl over 3cm of boiling water. The bowl must not touch the bottom of the pan. Don't touch the bowl without an oven glove – it will be hot!

5. Add vanilla essence, nuts and chocolate. If the mixture is dry add a tablespoon of milk. It should be quite soft.

6. Bake in a greased tin for about 20 minutes. It should be soft when it is ready. Do not overbake.

Cut it into squares while it is warm. Take it out of the tin when it is cool.

America at play

Americans work hard and play hard. Many like their leisure to be organised for them. So elaborate fun-fairs called amusement parks have been built.

America's first super amusement park was Disneyland in California. It is still one of the big favourites. Parents and children come here for anything – from meeting Mickey Mouse to riding in a space rocket. Disneyworld, in Florida is a newer and even bigger playground. The main attraction is a fairy-tale castle where you can meet the Seven Dwarfs.

The United States is a young country – only 200 years old – so Americans are often fascinated by very old things. One rich American bought old London Bridge and rebuilt it in the desert at Lake Haversu, Nevada. Tourists come a long way to see it.

Re-living America's history is another popular pastime. On Memorial Day, the last Monday in May, people come from all over the States to ride through the Rocky Mountains on the old Denver to Rio Grande railroad on its first run of the year. They book their tickets months in advance. Cyclists race the old steam train along a narrow ledge to Silverton. It is a steep ride – but the cyclists always win.

Many Americans also love sport. America is so big you can ski in the mountains or ride the Pacific surf at the same time of year. The jogging craze began in the States. Millions of Americans who are keen to keep healthy go jogging every day. They also go on long hikes or 'back-packing', often in National Parks.

Americans spend a lot of time and a lot of money on sport. Many schools have good sports facilities. American schoolchildren spend much more time on sport than European schoolchildren. It is often considered as

History lives on at Knotts Berry Farm, California as these tourists 'pan' for gold.

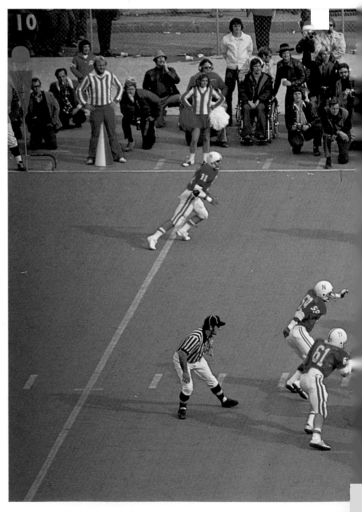

Cheerleaders and coaches urge their team to victory in a tough match of American football.

Up to speeds of 100 km per hour, rollercoasters career along their shiny tracks.

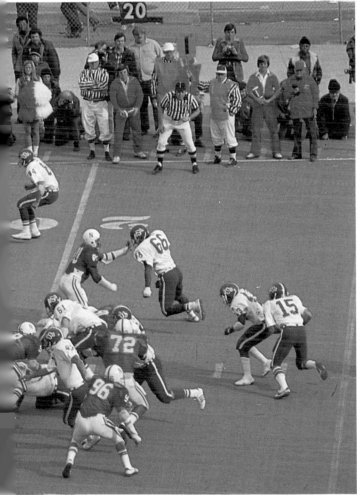

important as subjects like English or Maths. They can even win scholarships to college for baseball or basketball. When they do well in sport they are 'awarded the letter'. This means they can wear their school's initial on their sweatshirt.

Baseball is America's national game. It is very much like English rounders only much rougher and faster. American football is based on rugby. Players can run or throw the ball down the pitch. It is very different from European football which Americans call soccer.

Both baseball and American football are so rough that players have to protect themselves with special clothes. Footballers even have to wear crash helmets to protect their heads, ears and faces. On top of all the padding they wear bright team colours so that their supporters will recognise them. Footballers have their names on the sweatshirts, too.

New York

Washington DC is the capital of the United States but New York is the biggest city. It is also the world's tallest city. The heart of New York is Manhattan. As Manhattan is an island the city had to grow up, not out. Some skyscrapers are so tall that when you look up

Concrete canyon! The Manhattan skyscrapers seen from the top of the Empire State Building. The city is built on a grid system. All the streets have numbers so you can find your way about by counting blocks.

from the street you cannot see their tops. The highest building is the World Trade Centre. Its two towers are 415 metres high. The express lifts take only seconds to reach the 110th floor. From there you can see the whole of New York. But don't wear jeans, as they won't let you in!

Back on the ground the streets are packed with yellow cabs. The drivers are supposed to be the most knowledgeable of all New Yorkers. They may tell you that Manhattan was bought from the Indians by the Dutch for only $24 (about £12) in 1624. Since then millions of people from many countries have passed through New York in search of a new life. Steaming into New York harbour after many days aboard a cramped ship, their first sight was the Statue of Liberty, symbol of the free.

Gateway to a new life: arrival in New York

The *Hudson* was an old ship carrying mostly immigrants. All of them headed for America.

The morning of 30 December, 1913 in New York was clear and cold. There was snow on shore. I was on deck as we passed the towering Statue of Liberty. I was quivering all over. I glanced at the noisy crowd; people of perhaps a dozen nationalities pushing toward the rails, straining and stretching to catch a glimpse of the new country.

I had written to Stefan Radin, brother of my late friend Yanko, asking him to meet me on Ellis Island.

From the ship we were transferred to Ellis Island where I received a cable from Stefan that he was coming for me the next afternoon.

That day was an eternity. There were rumours that some of us would be refused entry into the United States and sent back to Europe. For hours I was in a cold sweat although my papers were all in order. Sewed in my jacket lining were 25 dollars which every immigrant needed before entering the country. Then I worked up a panicky feeling that I might get measles or smallpox. I had heard that hundreds of sick immigrants were quarantined on the island.

I spent my first night in America with hundreds of others, in an immense hall with four tiers of narrow iron bunks. I was assigned a top bunk. The blanket which someone threw at me was too thin to be effective against the blasts of cold air that rushed in through the open windows.

Late the next afternoon I was examined for entry into the United States. The examiner sat behind a great desk. On the wall above him was an American flag. The official had a stern voice and I had difficulty understanding his questions. When and where was I born? My nationality? Religion? Was I a legitimate child? What were the names of my parents? Was I an imbecile? A criminal? Why had I come to the USA? I was questioned on my finances and I produced the 25 dollars. What did I expect to do in the United States?

"And who is this person, Stefan Radin, who is meeting you here?"

I answered that Stefan was the brother of a dead friend of mine. Then the inspector waved me out of his presence.

I waited another hour. It got dark but finally Stefan was called into the room and asked to state his relationship to me. He answered that he was not related to me at all. Whereupon the inspector fairly pounced on me. What did I mean by lying to him? He threatened to return me to the Old Country. My heart pounded. But it occurred to me that the man must be mistaken.

It turned out that he had entered on my paper that I had declared Stefan Radin was my uncle. The examiner ordered me released.

Stefan picked up my bag. I had been denounced as a liar on my second day in the country. I was weak in the knees and just managed to walk out of the room and onto the ferry.

The little Ellis Island ferry bounded over the rough, white-capped waters of the bay toward Manhattan and the weakness soon passed. I was in New York, in America.

The inscription on the Statue of Liberty reads: 'Give me your tired, your poor, your huddled masses yearning to breathe free, the wretched refuse of your teeming shore. Send these, the homeless, tempest-tost to me.'

Celebration!

Every year on July 4 big celebrations are held all over the United States. People have a holiday and they decorate their homes with the American flag. Their flag is called the Stars and Stripes. It has 13 red and white stripes and 50 stars on a blue background. There is one star for each of the 50 states.

Americans everywhere are celebrating Independence Day. Two hundred years ago on July 4, 1776 their country declared its independence from Britain. Families go out to watch processions and bands marching through the streets. Children often wear red, white and blue and they carry flags and balloons. Some girls dress in satin shorts and sashes and march in the processions twirling sticks called batons.

All over the country on 4 July you will hear the blare of brass bands marching up and down the street. People across the land are celebrating the day their country broke away from the rule of the British.

They are called *majorettes*. In the evening there is a big firework display with rockets and more music. Everyone joins in the singing.

On October 31 American children celebrate Hallowe'en. They dress up as witches and ghosts, with ugly masks and big hats and go 'trick-or-treating'. They go from house to house and most of their neighbours give them a treat of candy (sweets). But if they are not given a treat they play a trick on the people who live in that house!

The fourth Thursday in November is called Thanksgiving. On this special American holiday children stay up late to join their families in a big Thanksgiving dinner. It is rather like Christmas. Aunts, uncles and grandparents all come to share roast turkey with chestnuts and sweet potatoes and pumpkin pie. They are remembering a great feast from long ago. The Pilgrim Fathers were some of the first English people to come and live in America. In 1621, to celebrate their first harvest in the new land, they sat down with the Indians to a feast which lasted three days.

At Hallowe'en people decorate their houses with carved pumpkins and candles to welcome trick-or-treaters. Beware you don't get tricked!

Index

The dark numbers tell you where you will find a picture of the subject

Publishing Manager:
Mary Tapissier

Editors:
Karen Adler
John Morton

Picture Research:
Caroline Mitchell

Production:
Rosemary Bishop

Factual Adviser:
Dr Stuart Kidd,
Bulmershe College of Higher Education

Cover Design:
Camron Design Ltd

Illustrator
Edward Carr

Teacher Adviser:
Eddy de Oro

The publisher wishes to acknowledge K Dallas Henderson for the use of *Why Cowboys Sing in Texas* by LeGrand Henderson.

Photographs:
Camera Press 14/15 (bottom)
J Allen Cash 7, 28/29, 38
Daily Telegraph 14/15 (top), 39, 43
Sally and Richard Greenhill 8, 12, 40/41, cover
Robert Harding 17, 44
Houston Sports Association 20
Alan Hutchison 26
International Photobank 13
Michael Ann Mullen 35
NASA 33
Photri 9, 10, 20/21, 45
Popperfoto 29, 34
David Redfern 27
ZEFA 10/11, 16, 24/25, 38/39

First published 1982
Macdonald & Co (Publishers) Ltd
Maxwell House
74 Worship Street
London EC2A 2EN
© Macdonald & Co (Publishers) Ltd 1982

ISBN 0 356 07103 0
Printed and bound by Henri Proost, Turnhout, Belgium

Cover: A lone cowboy out on the open range.

Introduction: All aboard at Disneyland, California